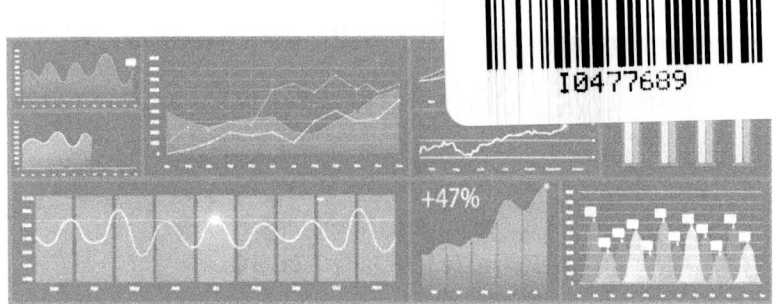

Practical Guide for Managers and Supervisors
# Performance through Stability

Revision 1

Eric M. Gatmaitan

Practical Guide for Managers and Supervisors
# Performance through Stability

Copyright © 2019-2024
Eric M. Gatmaitan
All rights reserved
Revision 1

ISBN-10: 1795213663
ISBN-13: 978-1795213660

Cover graphics © Sergeybitos

## About the Author

**Eric M. Gatmaitan** earned a master's degree in business administration with an emphasis on business information systems from Western Michigan University and a bachelor of science degree in industrial engineering with a minor in mechanical engineering from De La Salle University.

Mr. Gatmaitan is the author of the books *Manager's Guide to Lean and Performance*, *Building a Citadel: A Strategic Guide to Lean*, *Lean and Performance Driven*, and *Beginner's Guide to Crystal Report 2016*.

He was a faculty member at Western Michigan University teaching business information system. In the construction and manufacturing industries, he served as an industrial engineer, production supervisor, plant manager, and chief operating officer.

Mr. Gatmaitan leads projects and conducts training using industrial engineering and business management methods to enable organizations to operate faster, better, and easier. Areas of expertise includes business management, process optimization, quality systems, and performance management systems across various industries such as aluminum extrusion & anodizing, automotive, fabrication, healthcare, medical-device, pharmaceutical, and technology.

# Table of Contents

Introduction .................................................................1

**Chapter 1: Creating Stability** ...........................12

The Firefighting Index .......................................12

Process Development and Training Time.........13

Workflow Schematic ..........................................14

Process Validation .............................................15

A Unified Focus .................................................16

System Thinking .................................................18

Process Compliance...........................................22

**Chapter 2: Rapid Small Improvements**...........26

Eliminating Roadblocks .....................................27

Rapid Small Improvements.................................29

Capability and Capacity Improvements ............31

Kaizen Event.......................................................32

**Chapter 3: A Unified Approach** .......................33

Strategic Rationale ............................................33

Process Standards .............................................34

Focus on Purpose...............................................39

Performance Metrics and Standards ................41

Communication and Support Structure.............43

Management by Performance Objectives.........45

**Chapter 4: Discovery and Improvements........49**

The PDCA Cycle...............................................49

Embedding the PDCA Cycle..............................52

**Chapter 5: Visual Controls and 5S....................55**

5S is Not About Cleaning and Organizing ........57

Process Flow Control........................................58

Kanban for Inventory Management ..................61

5S Success.......................................................64

**Chapter 6: How to Create a Strategic Plan.......65**

Strategy Development .....................................65

Definition of Terms...........................................67

Strategic Planning Process...............................67

**Chapter 7: How to Develop a Business Process Map.......................................................78**

Elements of a Business Process Map ..............80

Process-Flow Diagram Symbols.......................83

Process Mapping Procedure ...........................86

**Chapter 8: How to Identify Key Performance Metrics .............................................91**

The Common Goal ...........................................91

The Planning Matrix.........................................92

Aligning Metrics ..............................................93

Cascading Strategic Metrics ...........................94

**Chapter 9: How to Conduct Kaizen Events ......99**

Process Overview ..............................................99

Event Preparation ...........................................101

Rules of the Game ...........................................102

Implementation Procedure ..............................103

**Chapter 10: How to Conduct an Objective Job
              Performance Review .....................110**

Design Considerations.....................................111

Rating System ................................................111

Components of a Job Performance Review ...115

Completing a JPR Form .................................121

Review Process ..............................................121

Linking JPR to Compensation .........................122

# Table of Contents

## *Introduction*

As a plant manager for a medical-device manufacturing company, I quickly saw the entire management team and technical staff engulfed in an environment of emergency issues throughout the entire supply chain. Our day is dominated by operational firefighting.

Attempting to get myself focused and organized, I made a list of eight action items to accomplish each day. Unfortunately, by the end of the day I see the same list untouched with a few more added.

During an operations review meeting, I asked the management team to take a quick survey.

# What percentage of your day is consumed by firefighting?

Everyone responded 100%. The entire staff knew we spent a lot of time firefighting, but not everyone at 100%.

This scenario is very common among managers and supervisors in organizations across all industries.

This book aims to help managers and supervisors develop operational process stability, predictability, and performance. The methods and techniques outlined in this book includes best operations management practices from the science of Industrial Engineering, Lean, and the Toyota Production System.

As an industrial engineer, I always consider the human factors to fully integrate a new method or change to the day-to-day operations. To sustain successful long-term implementation, the people performing the new process must experience an operation that is:

# Faster, better, and easier.

**Faster**  Will it increase efficiency?
**Better**  Will it improve performance outcomes?
**Easier**  Will it make the process simpler?

People will accept changes in the process if it will improve overall performance and make work life easier. The fundamental process to implement change must include the following:

1. Common goal.
2. Process standards.
3. Process compliance.
4. Understanding process variations, if any.
5. System corrective action.
6. Process improvements.
7. Performance management system.

**1. Common Goal**

A common goal defines purpose and the reliance of an organization for people to work together across all departments. Chapter 3 describes the process of linking strategic goals to each department and individual. It also describes a communication structure to monitor performance, identify areas requiring assistance, and provide resources to resolve performance issues.

Process improvement initiatives are identified as part of a strategic plan. Chapter 6 explains the process of developing a strategic plan which includes resource analysis, market analysis, strength-weakness-opportunities-threats (SWOT) analysis, objective development, strategy development, and the identification of projects or initiatives.

When organizations focus on the process to drive performance outcomes, they will need a performance dashboard to identify areas for improvement. Chapter 8 will help managers identify key performance metrics for every department and team in the organization. This chapter presents the strategic cascade approach linking financial and strategic performance metrics to every department and team.

## 2. Process Standards

Managers consider requirements for safety, quality, delivery, and cost when developing standard operating procedures (SOP). Compliance to the SOPs require training and follow-up coaching to assure (1) accuracy of the SOP and (2) training effectiveness. A strong emphasis on process compliance will help deliver desired performance outcomes.

Many of us experienced procedure writing as a cumbersome and painful process. Unlike conventional methods, Chapter 7 presents a simple and practical approach. To alleviate the difficulty of writing procedures, the method utilizes (1) process flow charts, and (2) an outline listing detailed requirements. It also explains the strategic cascade approach linking SOPs to the strategic, tactical, and operational activities of the organization.

Conventional procedure-writing methods, such as the Toyota Production System and Lean, are focused at the operational level. This approach is not the optimal approach at establishing process standards. Chapter 7 presents a more efficient and streamlined process using a top-down approach called the strategic-cascade.

Chapter 5 explains why most organizations get it wrong implementing 5S. See how 5S can help communicate process standards with minimal procedure writing and training.

## 3. Process Compliance

In a stable work environment, a manager can focus on rapids process improvements to enhance performance outcomes. A process-oriented organization requires high compliance and reliance on a process to deliver desired performance outcomes.

Chapter 1 provides the framework for process stability when launching a new product-service line or enhancing operational performance. This chapter helps a manager view an operation as a system and shows how process compliance can deliver operational safety, quality, delivery, and cost metrics.

## 4. Understanding Process Variations

Chapter 4 explains the Plan-Do-Check-Act (PDCA) cycle as a simple and effective process for continuous performance improvement. The PDCA cycle is a structured approach to prepare a work center to collect data, review the results, identify performance variations, and implement targeted corrective action.

The PDCA cycle can be used to simultaneously establish process compliance and implement process improvements.

## 5. System Corrective Action

The objective of system corrective action is to "correct" or adjust a process to minimize performance variations from resource elements, such as people, materials, equipment, and environment.

Typically, corrective action is initiated when performance falls short of expectation. Chapter 4 explains why it is just as important to apply corrective action when performance exceed expectations.

## 6. Process improvements

Managers can't do all the work to create a stable work environment. Chapter 2 outlines the basic concept of rapid small improvements involving everyone in the organization. This concept sets the tone for adopting the continuous improvement process as part of the organizational process and culture.

When an organization needs major process and/or performance improvements, Chapter 9 presents a practical Kaizen event procedure for the organization to deliver a concentrated effort to quickly improve an area.

## 7. Performance Management System

Organizations focusing on performance outcomes needs a performance dashboard to monitor progress and identify areas for improvement. Chapter 8 outlines the process of identifying key performance metrics for every department and team in the organization. This chapter also follows the strategic cascade approach linking financial and strategic performance metrics to every department and team.

Chapter 3 and 4 outlines the routine performance review process of the entire organization. The review process enables an organization to identify areas needing help, and how to allocate the necessary support for departments and teams to achieve their performance objectives.

Providing objective performance feedback is critical to encourage people to continue good performance or correct unfavorable performance outcomes. An objective job performance review (JPR) system is discussed in Chapter 10. It introduces a rating system based on the statistical normal distribution curve. This chapter also outlines the process of identify performance metrics, establishing a rating scale, and administering an objective JPR system.

**One Small Step at a Time**

After reading a chapter, I highly suggest implementing the concepts and methods in a small pilot area. This will give you the opportunity to learn, adjust, and perfect the implementation process.

Always focus on developing an effective process to deliver performance outcomes.

# Trust the process to deliver results.

On my first few months as a plant manager, I directed the management team and support staff to implement rapid small improvements to demonstrate the benefits of a process-oriented and performance-driven operation.

The rapid small improvements started the cultural change process. It communicated a uniform management approach at establishing process standards, monitoring performance, and implementing rapid small improvements.

Small incremental improvements are faster and easier to implement. Process improvements must produce a benefit greater than the overall effort of the implementation.

News of success spreads very fast in an organization. The management support staff gained confidence in every success. People in the organization are building trust with the changes, knowing that new initiatives will help them operate faster, better, and easier.

For the management team and technical staff, it is encouraging and fun to experience the improvements, the change, and knowing that you can make a difference.

I do hope you find this book a good resource to improve your firefighting index and enjoy witnessing the process of building a stable and high-performing workplace.

## Chapter 1: Creating Stability

The firefighting index is a good operational measure for workplace stability and predictability. With a low firefighting index, an organization can methodically conduct root-case analysis and implement effective solutions.

As a plant manager, I used the firefighting index to rally the management team and technical staff behind a common cause. Something that affects all of us at a personal level.

# What can we do to improve our life in this job?

One thing is certain, no one likes firefighting dominating their day. People want a stable work environment with a predictable work activity to show progress and improvements.

### The Firefighting Index

It is sad to see organizations across all industries accept high levels of firefighting as a fact of life that can't be changed. We need to realize that the firefighting index is not only a process stability metric, it is also a quality of life metric.

# Firefighting Index, a quality of life metric

Improving the firefighting index is no different than any other performance metric, such as on-time delivery or a customer satisfaction rating. A performance metric needs to be monitored, analyzed, and improved.

At a medical-device manufacturing site, the firefighting index was added to the strategic- and tactical-level performance scoreboards.

**Process Development and Training Time**

The largest issue confronting any organization is how to allocate time to reduce the 100% firefighting index.

At a manufacturing company, we scheduled a standard time for process development and training. A common time for the entire management team and technical staff to develop, train, and coach processes. In our case, we decided on a daily 1:00 pm to 2:00 pm schedule to establish process standards, coach for compliance, and implement improvements.

Each person created a list of top three firefighting activities. As a team, we identified root causes and implement corrective actions to reduce the firefighting index.

It took the management team and technical staff six months to lower the firefighting index from 100% to 65%. A year later, the firefighting index was reduced to a manageable 20% index.

## Workflow Schematic

Improving process stability requires analysis of the business process. Organizations providing products or services at any industry operate in an input-process-output workflow schematic.

A workflow providing a service or building a product is no different than a machine (process) that requires raw materials (input) to produce a product (output). The performance of the process is highly dependent on consistent quality and timelines of the input.

*Basic workflow schematic at any department, organization, or industry.*

Just like a machine, there are limits or tolerances, to input quality variations. Timely delivery and consistent quality of inputs help the process run faster to provide products and services.

Delivery of performance outcomes (output) are dependent on the design of the process and how the process is executed. During the design and development of a business process, verification activities are conducted to confirm compliance to planned or expected performance outcomes.

## Process Validation

During the development of a manufacturing line, equipment is tested to confirm compliance to operating specifications. In one case, it included an automatic equipment recovery from power outages. The validation activity included the simulation of a power outage by turning off the electrical circuit breakers while the equipment was running at full cycle. Power was then restored to observe the capability of the equipment to recover from a power outage.

Validation activities also provide operational data for use at establishing performance standards, such as productivity rate and uptime percentage.

For any process, consistent compliance to methods and standards are key to assure the highest performance outcomes. Process compliance helps to greatly reduce operational staff firefighting.

## A Unified Focus

An operations manager struggled to achieve a set of performance metrics. When the organization needed to increase delivery goals for the month, quality performance dropped. A campaign to improve safety resulted in a decrease in productivity. How can we achieve the entire set of performance targets?

The solution is communicating a simple performance-unifying focus:

# Process compliance.

Organizational policies, procedures, and work instructions are developed considering standards of performance for safety, quality, delivery, and cost.

Services and products in highly-regulated industries, such as healthcare, require high process compliance embedded throughout the entire supply chain, from vendors, work centers, and customers. This is also true for any organization seeking to deliver world-class quality products and superior customer service.

# Trust the process to deliver results.

Process compliance is the main driver at delivering performance outcomes.

## System Thinking

A process-oriented and performance-driven organization wanting to establish stability and predictability demands a methodical process at applying systemic corrective actions to greatly minimize or eliminate the occurrence of a performance deficiency. To better understand systemic improvements, we need to study the definition of a system. A system is:

# A group of inter-related elements working together toward a common goal.

The group of inter-related elements are resource elements needed by a business system to successfully execute the standard process. The inter-related elements are:

- ✓ People
- ✓ Machine
- ✓ Materials
- ✓ Methods
- ✓ Data

Everyone operates within a system. Examine your workplace and identify the people involved at supplying the necessary resources. Suppliers include external vendor, and internal departments.

| System Element | Resources Needed to Perform the job. |
|---|---|
| People | Vendors and internal departments providing resources. People required to perform the job. |
| Machine | Equipment, fixtures, and tools. |
| Materials | Raw materials, components and supplies. |
| Methods | Procedures, guidelines, and process checklists. |
| Data | Job specifications and product-service standards. |

For the machine element, identify the equipment, tools, and fixtures needed to perform the process. The material list includes raw materials, components and consumable supplies. Methods are documented instructions, guidelines, policy, and checklists providing guidance on how to perform the process. The data element consists of product-service standards, such as customer specifications and quality inspection standards. It also includes a work order specification listing what to do, how many, and the target due date.

Performance standards and expectations are defined for each resource element. For the resource element people, a job position candidate profile is required to determine education, training, and experience. Machine and materials require detailed performance specifications before they are purchased. Methods include verification activities embedded throughout the process of building a product or providing a service.

Verification activities are conducted to assure compliance to safety, quality, delivery, and cost standards. These performance standards define the common goal of the system.

A single performance-unifying effort simplifies the organizational message:

## Process compliance delivers performance.

Process standards are developed to generate the desired performance outcomes. It is ideal to conduct validation activities when developing or enhancing a business process. This activity confirms effectiveness of the business process to deliver the desired outcomes.

During the day-to-day operations, the management team and technical staff conducts process compliance audits to assure all system elements are working together toward the common goal.

A smooth-running operation is achieved by a supply chain of vendors, work centers, and delivery-service providers conforming to process standards.

In a workplace, activities can be categorized in two distinct groups. They are:

# 1. Day-to-day operations.
# 2. Process improvement.

Day-to-day operations provide the core business purpose of providing products and services to customers. Process improvement are projects to enhance day-to-day operations. The primary objective of a process improvement initiative is to establish process stability and predictability through process compliance.

## Process Compliance

Most people struggle allocating time for process improvement due to unplanned emergencies prompting people to engage in firefighting. The frequency of unplanned emergencies in the workplace is symptomatic of an unpredictable and unstable business process. A high level of process instability indicates low process compliance.

## Process Instability

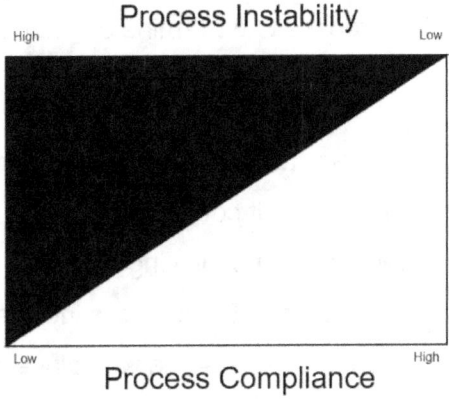

### Process Compliance

*Level of process compliance dictates level of process instability.*

Achieving high process compliance requires the development of process and performance standards. Process standards define the activities in a process, while performance standards are a set of expected outcomes.

Process and performance standards define the "rules of the game" for people to autonomously achieve goals and objectives.

After a training session, conduct follow-up coaching sessions to confirm training effectiveness and convey the importance of process compliance. Coaching sessions are also good opportunities for the management team and technical staff to examine the process to determine any need for improvement.

Process improvement doesn't necessarily mean changing the process, it could simply mean removing roadblocks at achieving process compliance. Examples of roadblocks include ergonomic issues, cumbersome workplace layout, unreliable equipment, or inconsistent supplier materials.

Process stability of the day-to-day operation provides time for managers to focus on meaningful and long-lasting process improvements. Without process compliance, process improvements are short-lived and unsustainable.

# Process improvement is useless without process compliance.

A chaotic environment is usually reliant on specific individuals to move the process forward rather than a process performed by everyone to achieve performance outcomes. Operating in a chaotic and emergency-filled work environment indicate the lack of organizational understanding on the importance of process compliance.

Process stability is continually challenged by the changing work environment and market demands. It requires the entire work team to be vigilant at applying process and performance improvements. The initial focus of any continuous improvement initiative must be establishing process standards and achieving process compliance. Process stability can be maintained with a methodical and data-driven approach to process improvement.

**Reference**

*Chapter 7: How to Develop a Business Process Map.*

## *Chapter 2: Rapid Small Improvements*

Work environments are never perfect, and people do their best on what they have at work. The management team and technical staff continually look for ways to make the process easier to produce better performance outcomes. This includes enhancing training, equipment reliability, consistency of materials, and ease of operation.

An organizational process improvement objective "make life easy" is a straight-forward and simple message to communicate. Everyone can agree and get involved at finding the easiest way at achieving performance standards.

# Faster, better, and easier.

Using performance objectives as a guide, everyone needs to be observant of the workflow, and generate ideas on how to operate faster, better, and easier. Working harder and faster is not a viable long-lasting solution.

Performance improvements must include ways to make it easier for people to perform the process consistently.

# Working harder and faster is not a solution.

### Eliminating Roadblocks

On my first job as a supervisor, I struggled to get the reluctant team to participate in daily team meetings to discuss performance metrics and solicit ideas on how to improve the process. I soon realized that I needed to adjust the purpose of the team meeting.

# How can we make your life easier to perform better?

With a new focus, the team started to warm up and started participating. Process issues were brought discussed and suggestions were flowing. We started an issue log to capture every observation and suggestion. The issue log was reviewed daily and validated by the team.

With an engaged team, I shifted my role as a supervisor to a support staff. The team was autonomously reviewing the process, performance outcomes, and applying corrective action. As the team discussed process and performance issues, they started to probe deeper into the rationale of the process standards and methodology.

## Question everything, nothing is sacred.

A scoreboard for operational concerns was posted and updated weekly to show the number of issues received, resolved, open, and oldest open. Aside from communicating the overall status of resolving team issues, the scoreboard also conveys the management commitment to listen and address issues brought up by the team.

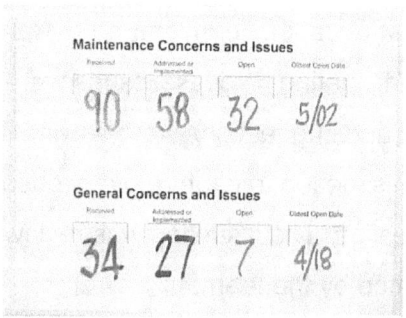

*Example: Issue Resolution Scoreboard*

## Rapid Small Improvements

As a production supervisor, my role was to provide operational and technical guidance. I relied on the operations staff to provide process-performance feedback and observations hindering the achievement of performance objectives.

Our daily team meeting is not a download of details from the supervisor. It is a candid discussion and analysis on how we can make operations easier to achieve performance objectives.

Nonconformances are quick and easy target for process improvements. These include noncompliance to procedures, nonconforming materials, equipment out of calibration, and inaccurate job data.

# Improve process compliance.

In some workplaces, people are encouraged to think big and make big leaps of innovation. Unfortunately, big ideas are hard to come by and face a lot of difficulty to implement. To engage everyone in the organization, focus process improvements to resolve the small and annoying issues.

# Think small

Small process improvements are generally easy to identify and resolve. This is a responsibility best assigned to the operational staff to autonomously identify and agree on the issues, develop a corrective action plan, and implement the plan. Supervisors doesn't need to manage this effort, they simply need to provide tactical guidance and logistical support.

An organization sensitive to shifting market needs and customer demands can deploy small improvements at a rapid pace. Organizations with a robust continuous improvement process involving all employees demonstrated outcomes of two improvements per person per month. A work team of ten people can implement twenty improvements a month, or the equivalent of 240 improvements a year. Imagine an organization with 1,000 people, that's 24,000 improvements a year!

Enhancing the operational details is best addressed by the work teams. They see the details of performing the process standard, encountering issues that slow down or hinder the process, and given the opportunity, they do know how to resolve the issue. People aren't involved at improving the process because the work environment doesn't allow them to get involved. □

## Capability and Capacity Improvements

The secondary objective of process improvement is to enhance the process to meet ever-changing work environment and market needs. As customer demand changes, the organization improves its capabilities to satisfy customer needs.

# Improve capacity and capability.

The organization may need to redesign the process, rearrange the layout of workplace, improve product design, purchase new equipment, or introduce new tools. This type of improvement affects either the capability or capacity of the process. Process capability includes the ability to provide tighter measured tolerances or the ability to rapidly produce smaller lot sizes. Improvements in process capacity are improvements at delivering a higher rate of work volume.

## Kaizen Event

Changes in the workplace may need to come big in one move, or gradually adapt through a series of rapid small improvements.

Big changes in the workplace can be addressed through a kaizen event, a concentrated effort to improve process capacity and capability in short period of time. Capacity improvements increase delivery volume, while capability improvements enhance safety, quality, delivery cycle, and cost features.

Typically, a kaizen event involves key personnel throughout the organization. They may include planners, buyers, operations supervisors, customer service, quality, facilities, and engineering. Kaizen events are big doses of improvements implemented in a day or week.

## Reference

*Chapter 9: How to Conduct Kaizen Events.*

## *Chapter 3: A Unified Approach*

The role of strategic management is to successfully navigate the organization through the marketplace to harvest opportunities and manage the threats. They develop strategies to move around market threats and take advantage of market opportunities to maximize profitability. The strategic-level management team provides directives and guidance to the organization, including process standards and performance standards. They also make sure the entire organization is cohesively working together towards a common goal.

### Strategic Rationale

Organizations routinely develop strategies to achieve performance objectives and identify project initiatives to support each strategy. Successful implementation of projects directly impacts the outcome of strategies that lead to the achievement of strategic plan objectives.

Project initiatives not listed in the strategic plan requires management review and approval to assure alignment to a specific strategy. Project initiatives aligned to a strategy clearly communicates the purpose and linkage to the overall organizational objectives. This also signifies the full support of the organization to provide resources to successfully implement planned projects.

## Process Standards

The conventional approach at establishing process standards, such as the Toyota Production System and Lean, dictate the development of work instructions at the operational level. Unfortunately, this approach encourages development of detailed work instructions for someone to read and perform. The result is a painful experience for a manager developing the procedure and a very confusing learning experience for a trainee.

# Writing procedures is not the goal.

In a top-down, strategic cascade approach, the strategic management team outlines the big picture business process using a simple flow chart. The example below shows the main steps of the process in rectangular boxes. The solid arrows point to the optimal or ideal path of the process. The dashed arrow lined are sub-optimal or not ideal paths of the process but are necessary for the organization to process.

To execute each main step, process details are required. A procedure document supplements the process flow charts. Each of the main step lists the detailed specifications or key points and identify the department or job position responsibility.

It is highly recommended organizations first outline the strategic process, such as order entry-to-shipping process, or proposal-to-cash process.

The approved strategic-level process identifies department responsibilities and how it impacts the organizational process.

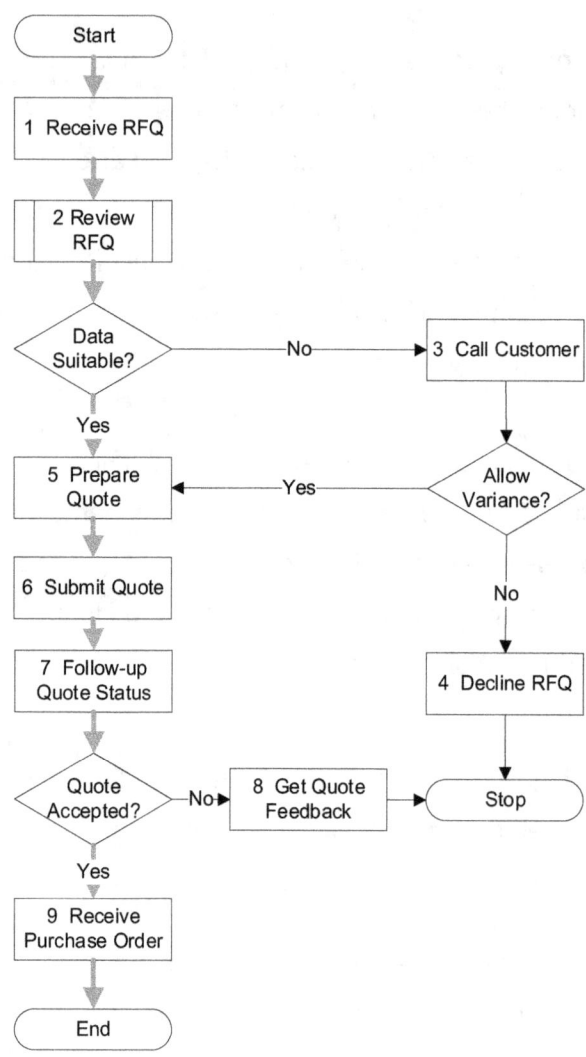

*Business process map using simple flow charting.*

| Main Steps | Key Points | Responsibility |
|---|---|---|
| 1. Receive RFQ | 1.1 Document in-bound date and time.<br>1.2 Existing or current customer. | Customer Service |
| 2. Review RFQ | 2.1 Product specification.<br>2.2 Part Volume.<br>2.3 Part design fit to process.<br>2.4 Fabrication.<br>2.5 Assembly. | Sales |
| 3. Call Customer | 3.1 Inquire on missing data.<br>3.2 Clarify customer specification. | Estimating |
| 4 Decline RFQ | 4.1 Contact customer.<br>4.2 Identify out-of-scope items. | Sales |
| 5. Prepare Quote | 5.2 Cost of process.<br>5.3 Cost of labor.<br>5.4 Cost of packaging material.<br>5.5 Coordinate pricing with accounting. | Estimating |
| 6. Submit Quote | 6.1 Verify accuracy and completeness prior to submission. | Sales |
| 7. Follow-up Quote Status | 7.1 For large volume quotes. | Sales |
| 8. Get Quote Feedback | 8.1 For large volume quotes | Sales |
| 9. Receive Purchase Order | 9.1 Direct Purchase Orders to Production Control.<br>9.2 Verify Purchase Order to Quote.<br>9.3 Attach print to Purchase Order | Customer Service |

*Procedure page outlining main steps, key points, and responsibility.*

With strategic-level guidance, departments develop tactical level (department-level) procedures. These procedures are drill-down details of the strategic-level process. Tactical-level procedures have the same format as the strategic-level procedures, containing main steps, key points, and assigned responsibilities.

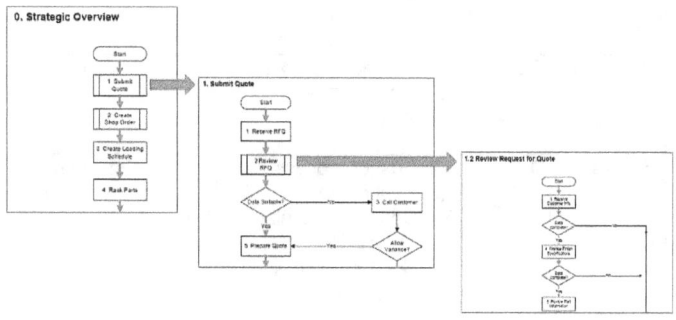

*Drill-down process flow charts.*

Strategic- and tactical-level procedures define the process standards. A well-executed strategic cascade approach to process standards significantly reduce the need for work instructions. A department-level procedure with high compliance are often enough for the operational staff to execute with minimal nonconformances. A work instruction is only developed on a per-need basis as part of a corrective action to eliminate, or significantly reduce, the occurrence of a process nonconformance.

## Focus on Purpose

The purpose of procedure development is to establish process standards and achieve compliance. Procedures are designed and developed for users, and not for any regulatory body. The procedure format must conform with the following:

✓ Easy to develop

✓ Easy to learn

✓ Easy to update

A procedure format that is easy to develop encourages managers and supervisors to establish process standards. An easy to learn format encourages the use of the document for training, coaching, and compliance monitoring.

Procedures that are easy to update enables the organization to continually improve the procedure to make it more relevant and useful for the people.

Industrial engineers use simple flow charting in every process optimization or streamlining project. The process flow chart is also known as a business process map, a very effective tool for analyzing a process, identifying areas for improvement, and illustrating the future state of the process.

Business process maps are easy to understand for people to use during training, problem solving, and process improvement activities. Shown below are example projects and performance outcomes using business process mapping.

| Organization | Performance Metric | Improvement |
|---|---|---|
| Fortune 100 Pharmaceutical | Financial month-end cycle time | 45 to 11 days |
| Custom Steel Casting | Order-to-ship cycle time | 16 to 5 weeks |
| Aluminum Anodizing | Order-to-ship cycle time<br>Ship-to-Invoice | 14 days to 6 hours<br>3 days to 1 hour |
| Printing | Job Packet Processing<br>Ship-to-Invoice | Two weeks to 2 hours<br>2 days to 1 hour |
| Medical-device | Work Center Setup Time | 12 hours to 20 minutes |
| Automotive | APQP Cycle Time | 45 days to 12 days |
| Fabrication | Steel Material Inventory | 35 days to 10 days |

*Improvements using business process mapping tool.*

## Performance Metrics and Standards

An approved strategic plan includes financial and operational performance targets. The management team assigns department responsibility for each strategic-level performance target. Using the strategic cascade approach, departments identify performance targets to assure achievement of strategic-level performance objectives.

Similarly, work teams in a department are assigned responsibilities to help achieve the department-level performance goals. If needed, work teams identify team-level performance standards relevant to their workflow.

A balanced set of performance metrics, also known as balanced scorecard, assures conformance to safety, quality, delivery, and cost standards throughout the workflow. Selecting six to eight performance metrics is a good starting point for a balanced scorecard. The number of metrics in a balanced scorecard may increase in time as the organization gains proficiency conducting routine performance reviews.

Shown below is an example listing of potential performance metrics covering the entire workflow and considering safety, quality, delivery, and cost performance categories. From this list, only six to eight items are selected for the balanced scorecard.

| | Input<br>Supplier | Process<br>Team | Output<br>Finished Product / Service |
|---|---|---|---|
| Safety | • Food safety | • Lost time safety<br>• Hazmat exposure<br>• Blind spot elimination | • Hospital acquired infections<br>• Hospital acquired pressure ulcer |
| Quality | • In-coming quality<br>• Patient triage | • Process compliance<br>• Near-miss medication errors | • Clinical outcomes<br>• Patient satisfaction |
| Delivery | • ER wait time<br>• On-time delivery<br>• Equipment availability | • Process Cycle Time<br>  ✓ From intake to discharge<br>• Capacity of resource elements<br>  ✓ Patient volume per staffing volume<br>  ✓ Length of Stay – Acute Care & ER | • Physician satisfaction<br>• Internal customer satisfaction<br>• Discharge summary integrity |
| Cost | • Purchase price variance | • Budget item compliance | • Revenue growth |

*Example list of performance metrics for healthcare.*

| | Input<br>Supplier | Process<br>Team | Output<br>Finished Product / Service |
|---|---|---|---|
| Safety | Hazardous material leaks | Accidents<br>Near misses | Customer complaints |
| Quality | In-coming Nonconformance | Defects produced | Customer complaints |
| Delivery | On-Time delivery | Schedule compliance | On-Time delivery |
| Cost | Purchase price variance | Productivity | Gross margin |
| Continuous Improvement | Corrective Actions Closed | Issues resolved<br>Suggestions | Corrective Actions Closed |

*Example list of performance metrics for manufacturing.*

## Communication and Support Structure

A top-down approach at communicating process and performance standards also requires a bottom-up approach for reporting performance feedback. Operational-level performance feedback includes performance outcomes, process issues, resource constraints, and support requirements.

The communication and support structure identify the work teams in an organization. Each work team is represented by a team leader, a lead job position or a three-month rotating team member assignment. Work teams routinely review performance data, analyzing outcomes, and implement corrective action, if necessary.

At the department-level, performance review includes the team leaders and the necessary cross-functional staff such as quality, engineering, information systems, human resources, and maintenance. Team leaders provide performance updates and relays issues requiring resources beyond the scope of the team. The role of the department manager is to assure alignment of team activities and assignment of responsibilities to support the needs of each team.

At the strategic-level management team, department managers provide performance updates, and relays department-level issues requiring support and resources beyond the scope of the department. The role of the site manager is to assure alignment of department-level activities and assignment of responsibilities to support attainment of department performance objectives.

*Communication and support staff structure.*

The structure above provides a framework for two-way communication. The management team use this structure to provide guidance and support, while the operational teams use this structure to communicate performance outcomes and relay process constraints.

A top-down strategic cascade at defining the organizational process and performance metrics provide a unified effort at achieving strategic objectives. The communication and support staff structure enable an organization to continually evaluate performance outcomes and implement corrective action, if needed. This is an effective structure for communication, monitoring performance, and allocating resources to areas needing help.

## Management by Performance Objectives

Managing a division with multiple departments and teams require the manager to focus on performance metrics and rely on visual controls. As a plant manager, I started my day walking around the facility conducting a quick pass-and-review of operations.

Performance charts with standards are maintained by each team, while visual controls made process nonconformances visible for everyone.

With pen and paper on hand, I made a list of observations to discuss at the daily operations meeting.

At the start of each shift, the entire facility is quiet. Everyone in the building attending a ten-minute team performance review, identifying issues, and planning for the day.

The management team and technical staff is spread out on rotation observing team meetings and providing technical advice and support.

The tempo and pace of the first two hours of a shift dictates the tempo for the entire shift. The entire support staff is on hand monitoring the shift start-up to assure a successful shift launch. No staff meetings are planned or schedule during this time.

# The first two hours dictate the tempo for the day.

Two hours after start-of-shift, a 45-minute operations performance review is conducted. Team leaders report performance outcomes, issues encountered, and support needs. The purpose of the operational meeting is to identify lagging performance metrics and allocate resources to quickly resolve issues.

Conducting operations performance reviews require process compliance to a fixed agenda and an analytical approach to problem solving. A simple agenda is shown below.

*Example Performance Review Agenda*
1. Planned time-off and work assignments.
2. Performance metrics review.
3. Concerns, issues, and suggestions.

**Individual Job Performance**

A comprehensive performance management system links the strategic-level performance metrics to every person in the organization. Job performance reviews (JPR) is a metrics-driven review linking individual performance to department and team objectives.

Everyone in the organization participates in the department- or team-level performance review. The routine department performance reviews provide data to individual JPRs. With this process, people are generally aware of their overall JPR performance prior to the scheduled JPR session with their supervisor.

**Reference**

*Chapter 6: How to Create a Strategic Plan.*

*Chapter 7: How to Develop a Business Process Map.*

*Chapter 8: How to Identify Key Performance Metrics.*

*Chapter 10: How to Conduct an Objective Job Performance Review.*

## *Chapter 4: Discovery and Improvements*

A process-oriented and performance-driven organization pursuing continuous improvement instills the values of discovery and learning. Work teams routinely reviewing performance data will discover new process failure modes, build a process capable of detecting nonconformances, and apply targeted corrective actions.

### The PDCA Cycle

The Plan-Do-Check-Act (PDCA) cycle is a generally accepted process improvement cycle across all industries, be it in the office or manufacturing environments.

The PDCA cycle is a simple process for work teams to independently monitor performance, identify issues, and implement corrective action. The role of a manager and supervisor is to provide technical support beyond the scope and capabilities of the team to improve the process.

*PDCA Cycle.*

Starting with the Plan phase, a work center develops the process standards, performance standards, and data collection process. Training and verification are conducted to assure process effectiveness prior to performing the work activity. In the Do phase, the work activity is performed along with some data collection.

The routine team performance review is an activity in the Check phase. Referencing expectations and standards, the team discuss observations and potential issues affecting performance. They also discuss ways to avoid bad performance, and just as important, how to replicate good performance.

| | |
|---|---|
| **Good** | **How can we do it again?** |
| **Bad** | **How can we avoid it?** |

Process improvement takes place in the Act phase. Improvements are targeted to eliminate inefficiencies and strengthen the business process. The newly improved process may include adjustments to training, equipment settings, material design, procedures, and data collection process. With the modifications implemented, the PDCA cycle starts over with the Plan phase.

In an organization of discovering and learning, managers assume an elevated role of business process developer, teacher, coach, and support staff. The manager develops the process and performance standards, builds process compliance, and provides resources for work teams to function autonomously.

## Embedding the PDCA Cycle

Integrating the PDCA cycle in the day-to-day activities requires the communication and support structure (see Chapter 4). Operational teams relay issues requiring assistance from the tactical-level departments. In turn, department issues requiring assistance are escalated to the strategic-level management.

*Communication and support staff structure.*

Every team and support staff perform the PDCA cycle as part the routine performance review process. Each group analyzing performance metrics, identifying issues, and continuously improving the business process.

The PDCA cycle is a simple data-driven and process-oriented process at building a culture of discovery, learning, and continually improving performance outcomes.

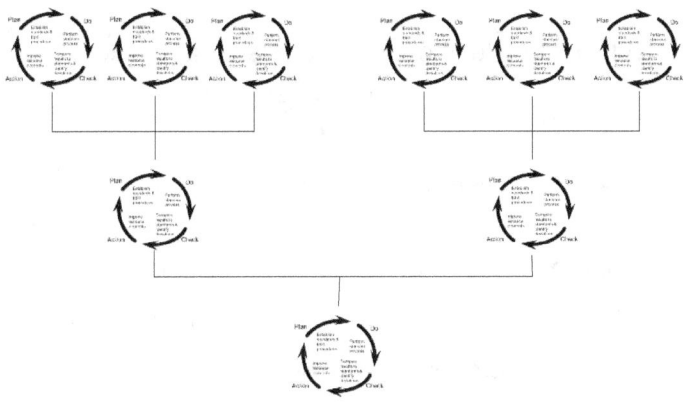

*PDCA cycle fully integrated in the organization.*

The PDCA cycle looks simple and yet, difficult to follow. It took me eight weeks to train myself to follow the process. It is so easy to jump into conclusions and make shoot-off-the-hip solutions.

# Be patient and follow the process.

## Case Study

Here is an exercise to demonstrate the virtues of patience and following the process.

**Situation** People always come up and ask "What do I do next?".

**Issue** Distracting and a waste of time.

**Solution** Train and coach the decision process to self-manage. Develop a visual decision process, if needed.

**Process**
1. Respond by asking "What do you think?".
2. Evaluate the response and coach the decision process.
3. Determine if a visual process, such as a checklist or flowchart, can help.

**Evaluation** How long does it take to gain 100% compliance to the process?

## *Chapter 5: Visual Controls and 5S*

The 5S of workplace organization was conceived by Toyota Production System (TPS) listing the five "S" elements of establishing and sustaining visual process standards.

The main purpose of 5S is to communicate process standards using visual aids, such as markings and signage. The use of visual aids enables an organization to minimize the use of written procedures, reduce training time, and make it easier to identify process nonconformances.

# Create the image
# that set the standards.

*5S improved creates the visual standards for process compliance.*

Lean 5S is the English-language adaptation of the TPS 5S as shown below.

| TPS | Lean | Description |
|---|---|---|
| Seiri | Sort | Throw away all scrap, trash and unrelated materials in the workplace. |
| Seiton | Straighten | Designate a place for everything, considering quick retrieval and storage. |
| Seiso | Shine | Routinely clean the workplace. |
| Seiketsu | Standardize | Establish 5S process standards. |
| Shitsuke | Sustain | Maintain process compliance. |

5S is an effective approach to communicate process standards, such as location of materials, next step of the process, when to stop a process, or signal the start of a process. A clean and organized workplace is a by-product of 5S.

## 5S is Not About Cleaning and Organizing

Unfortunately, organizations fail to realize the purpose and use of 5S. Most organizations use 5S primarily as a program for cleaning and organizing the workplace. People in the organization view this objective as a waste of time, non-productive, and a passing management fad.

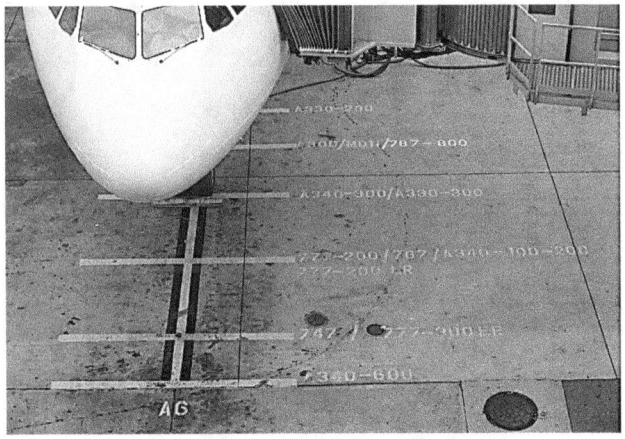

*Practical 5S implementation at an airport.*

A good use of 5S is shown above. The markings on the ground identify the target position of the nose wheel for different aircrafts. An aircraft positioned properly on the ground will align the aircraft door to the passenger jetway. This method simplified the jetway operation by eliminated the need to swing the jetway sideways and potentially damage the aircraft wing.

## Process Flow Control

Another form of controlling a process is by using flow control boxes, also known as Kanban squares in the manufacturing industry. A flow control box is a designated location for a specific material and quantity. A work center designates a flow control in-box for materials and an out-box for finished products. The flow control box specifies the maximum quantity to produce.

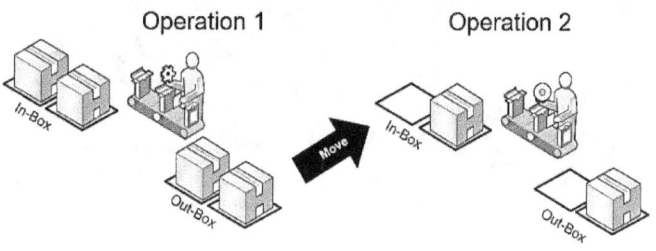

*Kanban squares used for flow control between two workstations.*

Materials can only be moved to the next operation when the in-box is empty. If the next operation in-box is full, the material stays in the outbox and signals the operation to stop.

# Only make what is needed.

In a flow-controlled process, operators are trained to work proficiently at multiple work centers. Cross-trained operators autonomously move to other work centers when the work center out-box is full.

*Work center flow control using Kanban squares.*

A work area with the staff moving around is also a safe work environment lowering the risk of repetitive stress syndrome. At a manufacturing facility with multiple work centers, we designated

Kanban squares to manage the workflow. The site manager decided to ignore the flow control boxes and instructed the staff to stay at a station and build inventory. Within a few months, operators were reporting aches and pains symptomatic to repetitive stress syndrome. Compliance to process controls were immediately re-established and within a few months, reports of aches and pains diminished significantly and was eventually eliminated.

The flow control box also applies to purchased materials. In-coming vendor materials must fit in the designated open flow control boxes. To do this, the material buying process considers the rate of material consumption and the delivery lead time to calculate the required in-coming material quantity. Vendor compliance to the specified delivery lead time and quantity is key at preventing material outages and excessive inventory.

Organizations with a complex supply chain requiring extensive coordination and control of material flow utilize an Enterprise Resource Planning (ERP) system. The ERP system is capable of electronically managing the supply chain using the flow control box concept.

It is common practice for organizations to exclude some material items from being managed by an ERP system. These items include common supplies such as copy paper, rags, lubricants, office supplies, pallets, and shipping supplies. These material items are often neglected resulting to an overabundance of supply or material stockouts. A stockout of these non-ERP controlled items often limit the organization to provide timely delivery of goods and services.

## Kanban for Inventory Management

A Kanban inventory system can help manage non-ERP material items. Kanban is a visual signaling method to prompt material users to notify buyers to purchase or release a specified quantity from a vendor. Like an ERP system, the calculated release quantity assures the appropriate in-coming material quantity to fill the open Kanban squares.

Kanban cards are attached to material stocking units, such as a case or pallet load. The Kanban card is taken off the material when using the first item from a case or pallet load.

*Kanban cards attached to material stocking units.*

The Kanban card taken off the material is placed on a designated location on the planning board. The designated location is marked by a "trigger" card that specifies the number of Kanban cards needed to signal a buyer to release material. The trigger card contains material information, such as use rate, purchase quantity, and vendor lead time.

*Kanban Planning board. Kanban cards placed under a trigger card.*

A well implemented Kanban system can reduce the occurrence of material stockouts and significantly reduce inventory levels.

At a metal fabrication company, raw steel occupies a large area best used for new equipment. After training and coaching the materials manager on the Kanban system, inventory was reduced by 45% and floorspace was cleared for new equipment.

## *5S Success*

During a 5S implementation, a manager asked, "How can we tell if we are successful with 5S?". My response:

*"5S is successful when the organization stops declaring a cleaning and organizing day each time a customer plans a visit."*

A successful implementation of visual controls and 5S requires clear communication of purpose and a practical application to a work environment. Minimizing the need to write detailed procedures, making it easy to train people, and improving performance are practical benefits people can quickly realize and fully participate. All of these, plus a clean and organized workplace.

To successfully implement 5S, focus on solutions to make people's life easier in the workplace. 5S is not a program for cleaning and organizing, it is the simplification of a process to operate faster, better, and easier.

## *Chapter 6: How to Create a Strategic Plan*

Projects and process improvement initiatives, such as Lean or Total Quality Management, must be linked to the strategic objectives of the organization.

In the development of a corporate strategic plan, programs, projects, and process-improvement initiatives are identified to achieve a corporate strategy. A top-down directive communicates a unified plan to execute specific project initiatives.

In this chapter, a strategic planning process is provided as a guide in developing a simplified strategic plan. Further research regarding the strategic planning process is highly recommended to improve the level of complexity of a strategic plan.

### Strategy Development

The strategic planning process is a widely used planning process with the goal of coordinating company resources to work in harmony at achieving a common objective.

The process, also known as corporate planning or CorPlan, requires analyzing current company capabilities, researching market dynamics, understanding the competitive arena, and gathering information on a wider array of factors, such as governmental, societal, and ecological concerns.

The planning process includes the identification of market opportunities-threats, development of strategies, and listing of projects and initiatives.

The process in this book outlines the major components and is starting point for developing a strategic plan. The level of simplicity or complexity of a strategic plan is on a per-need basis.

Start with a simple, straightforward strategic plan, and update it every six to twelve months. Gradually increase the level of complexity of the strategic planning process over the years.

## Definition of Terms

*Objective*: Something sought or aimed to achieve.

*Strategy*: The planned movement to position an organization in a favorable state.

*Program*: A project or initiative supporting the achievement of a strategy.

*Contingency*: A potential event that may alter or influence assumptions made in formulating strategies and programs.

## Strategic Planning Process

The top management team initiates the strategic planning process with a series of activities including compiling data, conducting research, and preparing the market data.

Research analysts will need to complete the market research before the executive-management team convenes a strategic planning session.

## Step 1: Analyze the Company Background

Research and compile the data requirements listed below. As much as possible, graph or chart the data.

### *History*

1. What is the story behind the start of the organization?

2. How did the business and product evolve?

3. What are the historical milestones of the organization? Include the high and low points.

4. What is the historical sales performance?

5. Is product mix a major consideration?

6. List other historical financial and/or operational data.

### *Organization*

1. What is the current organizational structure?

2. Is the current organizational structure adequate?

3. Is the organization appropriately staffed with qualified personnel?

4. Are the functional responsibilities defined?

5. Are performance indicators and objectives defined for each functional area?

## *Mission Statement Analysis*

1. What is the current mission statement?

2. What are the intended product and/or service benefits?

3. What are the target markets or industries?

4. Who are the target end-user customers?

5. Is there a need to update the mission statement?

## *Analysis of Company Activities*

1. What are the current product and/or service benefits?

2. What are the best products and/or services?

3. What are the worst products and/or services?

4. What markets and industries are being served?

5. Who are the current end-user customers?

6. Is the business process adequately defined and functioning as intended?

## *Resource Assessment*

List the current capabilities and limitations of the company using the matrix below.

| | Capabilities | Limitations |
|---|---|---|
| Conceive and design | | |
| Market | | |
| Manufacture the product | | |
| Provide the service | | |
| Distribute the product | | |
| Provide customer service | | |
| Manage the business process | | |

## Step 2: Identify the Strengths and Weakness

Identify the strengths and weakness as viewed internally (within the organization) and externally (as viewed by customers and competitors).

|  | Strengths | Weakness |
|---|---|---|
| Internal |  |  |
| External |  |  |

## Step 3: Define the Arena of Competition

Conduct market and competitive analysis to provide the landscape of the competitive arena. This will define the target market profile and its characteristics.

1. What markets are currently being served?

2. What are the target markets?

3. Who are the competitors?

4. What products are provided to each market?

5. How does the company compete in the market?

6. What services are offered to each market?

7. What are your competitors' advantages?

8. What are your competitors' disadvantages?

Compile the data gathered in the matrix below.

|  | Market 1 | Market 2 |
|---|---|---|
| The competitors |  |  |
| Product group |  |  |
| Method of competition |  |  |
| Services offered |  |  |
| Competitor advantage |  |  |
| Competitor disadvantage |  |  |

## Step 4: Conduct an Environmental Analysis

### *Industry Analysis*

Conduct an industry analysis outlining the general industry performance, trends, emerging markets, declining markets, industry threats, and opportunities.

### *Economic Concerns*

Identify local, regional, state, or US economic factors that may impact the target markets. Also, include the global economic factors that may impact the target markets.

### *Governmental Concern*

Identify any laws that may impact the target markets.

### *Technological Environment*

Identify new technology that may influence the dynamics of the market, end-users, product quality, cost, and/or manufacturing methods.

### *Societal & Ecological Concerns*

Identify any potential public concerns of product use and its impact to the ecological environment.

## Step 5: Identify Market Opportunities and Threats

Examine the competitive market, market research, and environmental analysis. Identify the opportunities and threats for each target market.

|  | *Market 1* | *Market 2* |
|---|---|---|
| Opportunities |  |  |
| Threats |  |  |

## Step 6: Define the Strategic Objective

Clearly define the objective of the organization for the time period covered by the strategic plan. The objective must identify the performance metric, the current state, the future state, and the completion date. An example of a strategic objective is listed below:

> *Grow sales from $5 million in 2019 to $15 million by 2021 while maintaining net income at 10 percent.*

## Step 7: Develop Strategies

Develop strategies to support the achievement of the objective. Strategies are big movements within the organization and the target markets. Examples of strategies are:

1   *Penetrate Market 1 and capture 5 percent market share.*

2   *Expand base account sales in Market 2 by 12 percent.*

## Step 8: Identify Programs, Projects, and Process-Improvement Initiatives

Identify initiatives and the target implementation dates for each strategy.

1   *Penetrate Market 1 and capture 5 percent market share.*
   - *New product release Spring 2020*
   - *Manufacturing cost reduction, 10 percent by October 2020*

  2   *Expand base account sales in Market 2 by 12 percent.*
   - *Reduce product price by 5 percent by July 2020*
   - *Release expanded product line offering by 20 percent by May 2020*

## Step 9: Develop a Contingency Plan

Identify critical assumptions behind each strategy. Examine assumptions in the market analysis, identification of market threats/opportunities, and the environmental analysis. Answer the questions below to outline the contingency plan.

1. Identify critical issues or events that could possibly hinder the strategy and program implementation.

2. What are the alternate strategies and programs?

3. What are the trigger points to implement the contingency plan?

## Step 10: Approve and Release the Strategic Plan

Publish the strategic plan as a formal document for the entire organization to follow and execute. Route the strategic plan for management review and approval.

## Step 11: Monitor Compliance and Data Integrity

The strategic plan is intended to be reviewed on a routine basis for changes in market data and plan assumptions. Data is continually compiled in preparation for the next strategic planning session.

## Chapter 7: How to Develop a Business Process Map

A business process map is a good analytical tool to understand the processes in an organization. I use business process mapping on every optimization project to improve performance outcomes. It is the quickest method to understand the current business process and swiftly identify areas for improvement.

In one case, an organization wanted to optimize the cycle time of the entire business process, from order entry to receiving customer payment. After eighteen months of conventional mapping efforts, the continuous improvement team was stuck at the order entry phase. The organization needed help and decided to use the business process mapping method in this chapter. Within six weeks, the entire process was documented and areas for improvement were identified.

Unfortunately, the typical approach to process mapping and documentation is focused at the operational level. This chapter presents a simple and logical approach starting with the strategic level and drilling-down to the tactical- and operational-levels. This approach is called a strategic cascade.

The process mapping methodology in this chapter was developed using a blend of industrial engineering, information systems, and instructional design principles. The process map consists of a (1) process-flow diagram, and (2) procedure page.

The process-flow diagram is created using a highly structured approach to outline the optimal and sub-optimal paths of a business process. An optimal path is the favored and most efficient process flow. The sub-optimal path is least favored but are necessary in the business process. Examples of sub-optimal paths include placing a work folder on-hold for further review, rework, and implementing corrective action.

The process-flow diagram is complemented by a procedure document. It lists the main steps of the process flow along with key points and assigning responsibility.

It is highly recommended to document the business process maps before writing work instructions. Work instructions complement process maps when detailed step-by-step procedures are necessary. In most cases, high compliance with a business process map minimizes the need for detailed work instructions.

## Elements of a Business Process Map

The completed business-process map contains (1) a process-flow diagram and (2) a procedure section.

The process-flow diagram shows the sequence of events and the logical flow. The most efficient path is clearly visible as a straight path flowing down, while the least desirable, and often non-value-adding, activities are shown flowing sideways.

# Example Process-Flow Diagram

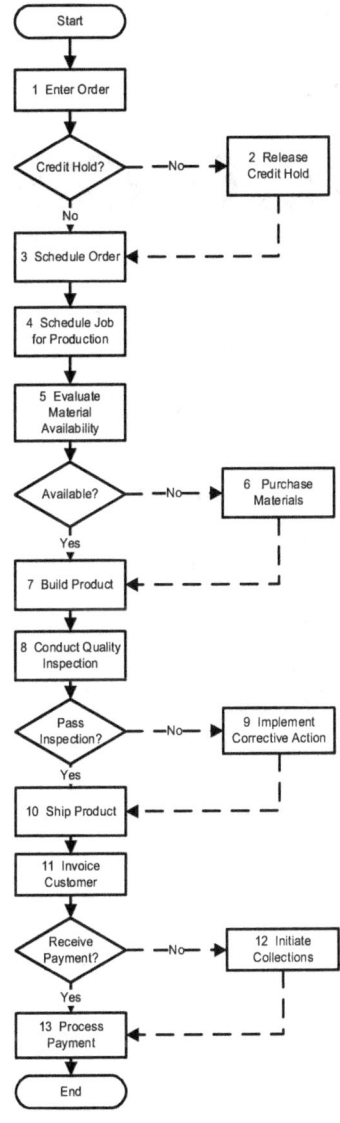

The procedure section lists main steps, key points, and responsibility.

*Example Procedure Section*

| Main Step | Key Points | Responsibility |
|---|---|---|
| 1 Enter order | 1.1 Check for completeness.<br><br>1.2 Write O/E number on PO package. | Customer Service |
| 2 Release credit hold | 2.1 Supervisor approval required.<br><br>2.2 See SOP-578. | Financial Services |
| 3 Schedule order | 3.1 Enter work order.<br><br>3.2 Identify customer priority code. | Customer Service |
| 4 Schedule job for production | 4.1 Sequence active jobs. | Planning |
| 5 Evaluate material availability | 5.1 Verify MRP requirements.<br><br>5.2 Inspect A items. | Purchasing |

## Process-Flow Diagram Symbols

For simplicity, limit the use of flow-charting symbols to the Terminator, Process, Line Connector, Decision, and Connector symbols.

A *Terminator* symbol indicates the starting point and ending point of a process. Terminator symbols include Start, Stop, and End.

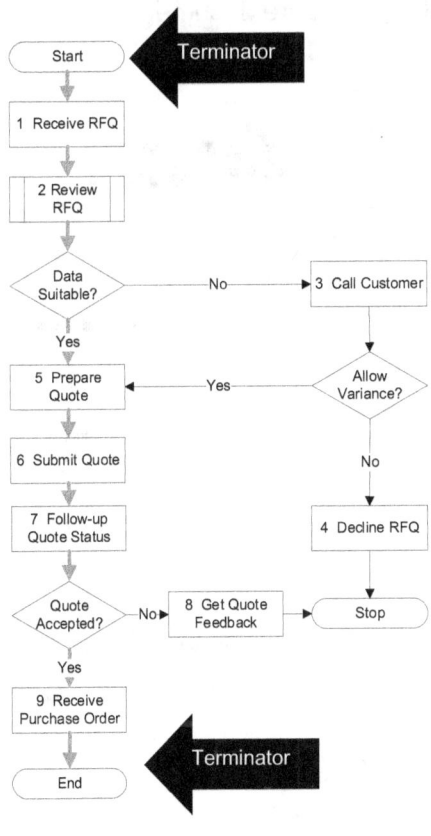

The *Process* symbol is represented by a rectangle using the format below and describes a main step.

*<Action> <Object>*

Examples:   Schedule Work Order
Assemble Product
Prepare Shipment

Keep the main step short and simple. Details will be listed in the procedure document.

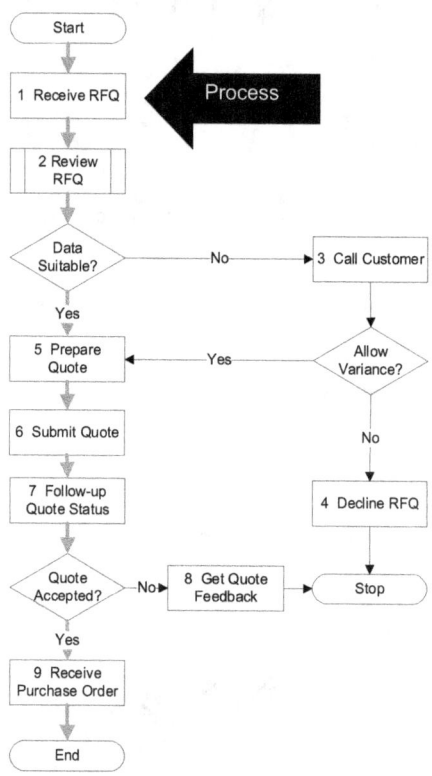

The Line Connector directs the process pathway from one symbol to another. Line connectors are labeled when directing multiple pathway options.

A Decision symbol is a junction where the process is routed based on a decision, result, or output. The preceding Process symbol generates an outcome for the Decision symbol. Line connectors identify the pathway options.

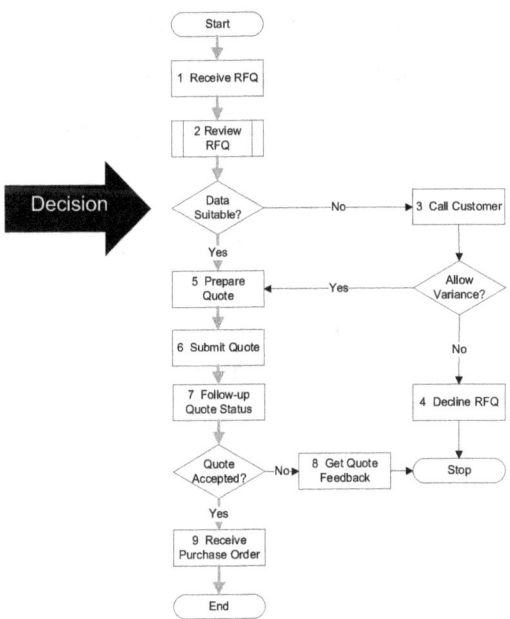

A *Connector* symbol is a utility that maintains simplicity and clarity in the process-flow diagram. Use this to eliminate overlapping line connectors, and link one process to another. Identify each connector numerically.

## Process Mapping Procedure

### Step 1: Develop a Process-Flow Diagram

Outline the business process at a very high level or strategic view. List the main steps only. Use a flow-charting software, such as Microsoft Visio, to produce a legible diagram. Here are the process-flow-diagram guidelines:

- Keep the process map simple and easy to understand.
- Use connectors to eliminate overlapping lines.
- Limit the process map to a single page.
- Number each process symbol.
- Develop a straight-line flow indicating the best-case scenario.
- Direct non-ideal pathways to the side.

## The Optimal or Ideal Flow

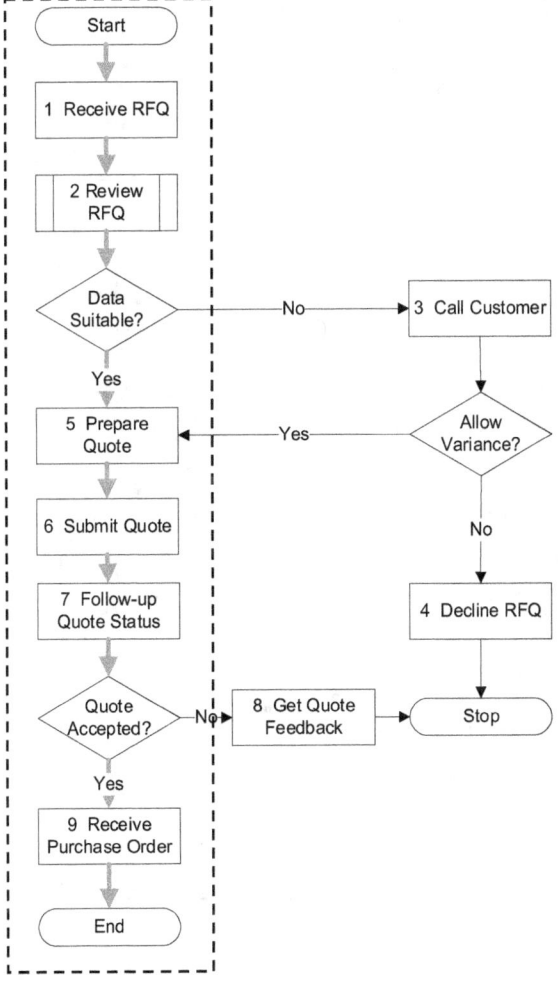

## *Resource-extensive and Undesired Processes*

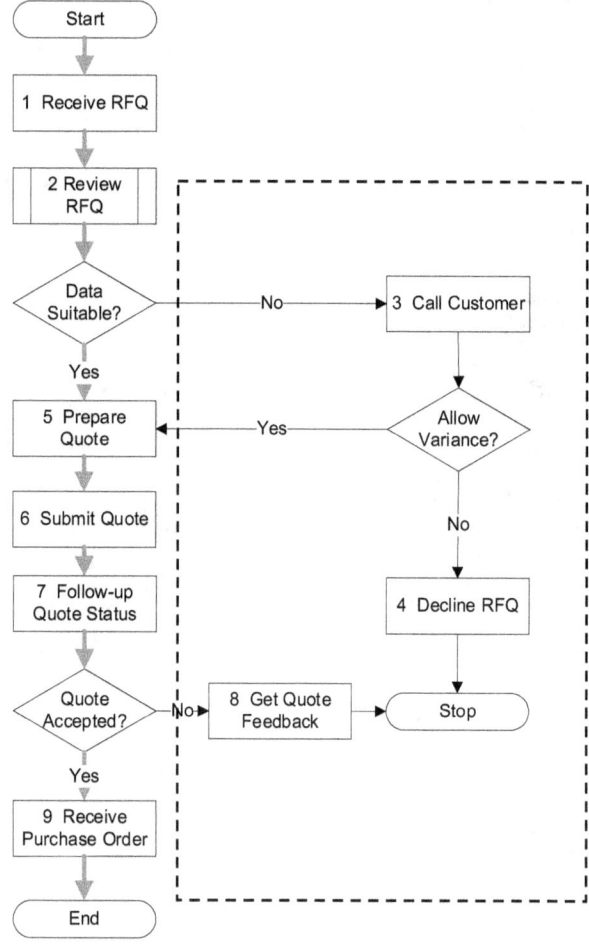

## Step 2: Verify the Accuracy of the Process Map

Enlist the expertise of end-users to validate the accuracy of the process-flow diagram. Monitor the current process and validate the process-flow diagram.

## Step 3: List the Main Steps in the Procedure

Copy the main steps listed in the process-flow diagram, excluding the decision symbol text.

## Step 4: List Key Points

Identify a maximum of eight key points for each main step. These key points may include the following:

- Safety precautions
- Assembly specifications
- Verification requirements
- Product handling and care tips
- Documentation requirements

## Step 5: Assign Responsibility

Identify the job function or department responsible for executing each main step. Multiple departments may be listed for a specific main step.

## Step 6: Route Document for Approval

Apply document control notations as specified by
the quality-system procedures and route the
document for approval.

## Step 7: Conduct Training

When training on the process map, state the
objective and end-result. Use the process-flow
diagram to explain the logical flow. Reference the
procedure section to highlight key points and
responsibilities.

## Step 8: Develop Tactical-Level Process Maps

Each main step in the strategic-level process map
is a potential area for developing a tactical-level
process map. About 70 percent of the main steps
will require a tactical-level process map.

## Step 9: Develop Operational-Level Process Maps

Operational-level process maps are developed on a
per-need basis. An estimated 25 percent of tactical-
level main steps require an operational-level
process map.

## Chapter 8: How to Identify Key Performance Metrics

### The Common Goal

Identifying key performance metrics is similar to building an instrument panel indicating the performance status of suppliers, team, and customers throughout the entire process.

*Basic workflow schematic at any department, organization, or industry.*

An organization with an extensive instrument panel showing the perfomrance status of every team, department, and division caneasily identify areas where help and resources are needed the most.

As discussed in Chapter 1, business processes across all industries and departments conform to the input-process-output schematic. External vendors and internal departments function as suppliers to a process. They provide materials and resources as input for a work center to produce goods and services as an output.

Each step of the input-process-output workkflow are broad goal categories. They are safety, quality, delivery, cost, and continuous improvement.

## The Planning Matrix

A planning matrix, shown below, is a helpful guide at identifying potential performance measures. The column header represents the input-process-output workflow, and the row headers list the broad goal categories.

| | Input (supplier) | Process (team) | Output (finished product) |
|---|---|---|---|
| Safety | Hazardous material leaks | Accidents and near misses | Stack height compliance |
| Quality | Defects received Firefigthing Index | Defects produced Firefigthing Index | Defects shipped |
| Delivery | On-time delivery | Schedule compliance | On-time delivery |
| Cost | Purchase-price variance | Productivity | Purchase-price variance |
| Continuous Improvement | NCR-CAR | NCR-CAR suggestions | NCR-CAR |

*Planning matrix for identifying potential performance measures*

Examine the input stage of the workflow.The potential pereformance measures are identified for each broad category -  safety, quality, delivery, cost, and continuous improvement. The same is done for the process and output stages.

For starters, the area supervisor selects between five to eight key performance metrics. These performance metrics represents the control panel displaying performance data.

## Aligning Metrics

Organizational focus on performance requires a top-down cascade of performance metrics. Like the process mapping approach in Chapter 7, performance metrics use the strategic cascade drill down of strategic performance metrics.

Performance metrics and diagnostic measures are more meaningful when they are linked throughout the organization. The cascade of performance metrics, and business process maps create the basis for organizational discipline and purpose. It links every person to a common goal and process.

## Cascading Strategic Metrics

*Strategic-Level Metrics*

### Step 1: Identify the Financial Metrics

The executive-management team reviews the profit-and-loss (P&L) statement and assigns department responsibility for P&L line items and general ledger accounts.

### Step 2: Identify the Strategic Plan Metrics

Examine the programs, projects, and process-improvement initiatives listed in the strategic plan. Identify performance metrics that reflect the execution of initiatives, such as a project summary report. Diagnostics measures may be used to indicate the effectiveness of a program.

### Step 3: Identify Quality Management System, Regulatory Affairs, and Safety Metrics

Incorporate metrics for quality management system review, regulatory affairs, safety, and other corporate concerns. Limit the review to strategic-level metrics only. The details of nonconformances or audits are delegated to tactical- and operational-level reviews.

## Step 4: Define Strategic-Level Metrics and Sources of Data

Create a listing of performance metrics by responsibility. A short definition of the performance metric clarifies where and how the performance data is generated. By identifying the data source, an organization will continually refine the data collection process to assure timely delivery and accuracy.

## Step 5: Schedule Routine Strategic-Level Management Review

Set a routine for the executive-management team to review the performance metrics by area of responsibility. Each manager should review the assigned performance metric, highlight variances from the plan, and identify the recommended action plan to correct unfavorable variances. A separate project-review session may be scheduled, if necessary.

*Tactical-Level Performance Metrics*

## Step 6: Assign Department-Level Responsibility

The strategic-level manager meets with the subordinate tactical-level managers to review department-performance measures. Assign responsibility for each performance metric. Multiple tactical-level managers may be assigned to the same performance metric.

## Step 7: Identify Tactical-Level Diagnostic Measures

Each tactical-level manager identifies diagnostic measures for the assigned strategic-level performance metric. Diagnostic measures are detailed data sets that align to the attainment of strategic-level performance objectives.

## Step 8: Identify Quality Systems, Regulatory Affairs, and Safety Metrics

A detailed examination of compliance and system requirements is conducted at the tactical level. Each nonconformance is reviewed, and each corrective action is monitored to completion.

Diagnostic measures will include the number of (1) items received, (2) items closed, (3) open items, and (4) date of oldest open item.

## Step 9: Define the Department-Level Metrics and Sources of Data

Create a listing of performance metrics, sources of data, and responsibility.

## Step 10: Schedule Tactical-Level Reviews

Schedule a routine review of tactical-level metrics with all managers, supervisors, and support staff. Every member reviews their assigned performance metric, highlights variances from the plan, and identifies the recommended action plan to correct unfavorable variances. The details from this review prepares the department manager for the strategic-level metrics review.

*Operational-Level Performance Metrics*

## Step 11: Identify Operational-Level Diagnostic Measures for Each Work Team

The tactical-level manager meets with the subordinate operational-level supervisors to review the assigned operational-level performance measures. The manager assigns responsibility for each performance metric and diagnostic measure. The same performance metric mat be assigned to multiple supervisors and team leaders.

## Step 12: Identify Quality Management System, Regulatory Affairs, and Safety Metrics

For the operational team, the primary focus is compliance. Consistent with the strategic- and tactical-levels, each team will monitor the number of (1) items received, (2) items closed, (3) open items, and (4) date of oldest open item.

## Step 13: Define the Work Team Metrics and Sources of Data

Create a listing of performance metrics, sources of data, and responsibilities.

## Step 14: Schedule Operational-Level Reviews

In general, work teams review performance data at a reasonable cycle when meaningful data can be collected. Most organizations can accommodate a daily team performance review limited to fifteen minutes following a strict meeting agenda.

## Chapter 9: How to Conduct Kaizen Events

## Process Overview

A kaizen event is a fast-paced process improvement activity deployed at a targeted area. The kaizen event process presented in this chapter follows the Plan-Do-Check-Act (PDCA) cycle.

Multiple cycles are necessary for a kaizen event. The first cycle measures the baseline to validate historical data. In some instances, baseline data may differ significantly from historical data. This is due to higher process compliance along with a phenomenon called the Hawthorne Effect. The Hawthorne Effect occurs when a closely monitored activity causes people to modify their behavior and alter performance data.

Process analysis and improvements are made using data and observations gathered from each kaizen cycle. All members of the operational team and support staff reviews the data, develops an improvement plan, and implements the plan in preparation for the next cycle.

The second cycle will typically show the largest performance-metric improvements. The succeeding cycles will yield minimal improvements relative to the second cycle. Here is the profile of observed performance improvements for a Kaizen event, with the first cycle as baseline.

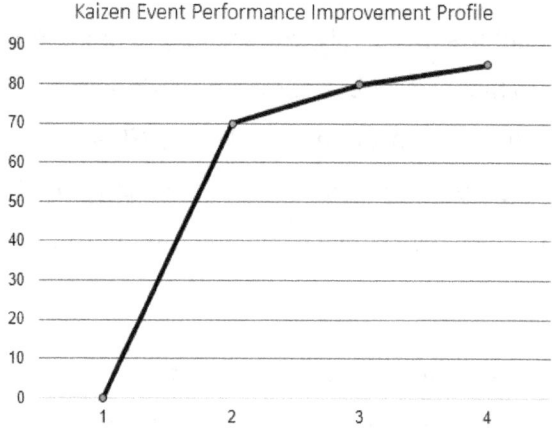

Kaizen Event Performance Improvement Profile

## Event Preparation

To sustain long-term effectiveness and compliance, a thorough preparation of all system elements is required.

*People:* All members of the operational team and support staff are briefed on the Kaizen event's objective, scope, and general plan. Involve all members in the detailed planning, preparation, and implementation. Develop a staffing plan and member responsibilities.

*Machines:* Create a checklist of fixtures, machines, equipment, and tools. Make sure the items are available for the event.

*Materials:* Create a master list of parts and materials required. Allocate, identify, and set aside the quantities.

*Methods:* Develop a big-picture process map showing the general process within the scope of the Kaizen event. Review the current data collection process and enhance the process for quick data retrieval if necessary.

*Data:* Use key performance metrics and process data to describe the current situation and problem statement. Compile the master records that will be used for the event. Master records contain the product or service specifications, drawings, and standards. Compile the necessary forms for a product or service-history record.

## Rules of the Game

Create a simple list of rules to maintain the integrity of the Kaizen event. The process must propel itself without any artificial effort, guidance, or support.

Stress the importance of following the procedure and the importance of performing the task at a normal pace. Focus on process compliance and not speed. Use flow control boxes (Kanban squares) to highlight bottlenecks and line balance issues.

The technical support staff will observe the process during the kaizen event and not interact or help during the event cycles.

Here is a summary of the Kaizen event rules:

- Perform the process and functions as specified.
- Execute with a normal pace—do not rush.
- Stop when flow control boxes are full.
- Support staff can observe the process but not get involved by helping the operational staff.

## Implementation Procedure

*PDCA: Plan Phase*

### Step 1: Define the Objective

The objective contains a statement of the current state and the target future state, such as "Improve the service-packet-completion cycle time from six hours to two hours."

### Step 2: Gather Current Process Data

Compile and study standards, specifications, historical data, and performance metrics. Draw a process map and summarize the key points for each main step. Gather process cycle times for each workstation, if necessary.

## Step 3: Plan the Kaizen Event

Define the scope of the Kaizen event, outlining the process, products or services, and the total number of units to process or produce.

Identify performance metrics to track the overall system effectiveness and diagnostic measures to monitor details of the process. Examine the current data-collection process and verify that all performance data are collected. Design a data-collection process, if necessary, to quickly gather new data points.

## Step 4: Prepare for Cycle #1

Prepare the work area and verify the material quantities required and equipment readiness. Examine the layout of the work area, and designate flow control boxes.

Develop or update procedures, if necessary. Verify training competencies and retrain people if necessary.

Set up the data-collection sheets and performance charts in an area close to the Kaizen event. This area will be used by the entire team to review the data, analyze it, and develop process improvements.

Conduct a trial run to verify that all elements of the system are ready. In a production setting, building two or three units may be adequate.

*PDCA: Do Phase*

**Step 5: Run Cycle #1 for Baseline Data**

Review the kaizen event rules prior to starting the cycle. Provide last-minute instructions to assure the integrity of the data and the entire event cycle. The team should focus on process compliance.

Collect production data and have the support staff gather observations pertaining to line balance, equipment or material issues, process compliance, and tempo.

*PDCA: Check Phase*

## Step 6: Examine Quality and Performance

Conduct a thorough examination of the products and/or services provided. Document detailed quality and performance outcomes.

## Step 7: Prepare Data for Analysis

Compile all data and present it in both detailed and summary formats. As much as possible, present data in graphs and charts.

## Step 8: Analyze the Performance Data

The Kaizen event leader presents the data to all members of the operations and support staff. Start with the overall performance metrics, and drill down to diagnostics measures.

The event leader should encourage feedback from all participants to identify issues and share observations.

*PDCA: Act Phase*

## Step 9: Implement Corrective Action

Prioritize the performance issues. Develop a corrective-action plan targeted to improve the top performance issues. Engage the operations staff in the development and implementation of the corrective-action process.

*PDCA: Plan Phase*

## Step 10: Prepare for Cycle # 2

Prepare the work area and verify material availability and equipment readiness. Update the process map, procedures, and documents affected by the improvements. Conduct training and coaching to ensure compliance with new processes.

Conduct a trial run to verify all elements of the system are ready.

*PDCA: Do Phase*

## Step 11: Run Cycle #2

Review the kaizen event rules prior to starting the next cycle. Provide last-minute instructions to assure the integrity of the data and the entire event cycle. Have the team focus on process compliance.

Collect production data and have the support staff gather observations pertaining to line balance, equipment or material issues, process compliance, and tempo.

*PDCA: Check Phase*

## Step 12: Examine Quality and Performance

Conduct a thorough examination of the products produced and/or services provided. Document detailed quality and performance outcomes.

## Step 13: Prepare Data for Analysis

Compile all data, and present it in both detailed and summary formats, comparing it to the previous run cycle(s).

## Step 14: Analyze the Performance Data

Review the run-cycle data and compare it to the previous run cycle and the planned objectives. Start with the overall performance metrics, and then drill down to diagnostics measures and detailed data points.

*PDCA: Act Phase*

## Step 15: Implement Corrective Action

Prioritize the performance issues. Develop a corrective-action plan to improve the top performance issues.

## *PDCA: Next Run Cycle*

Continue to run multiple PDCA cycles until the desired performance outcomes are achieved.

## *Chapter 10: How to Conduct an Objective Job Performance Review*

Most job performance reviews are troublesome and awkward for both the supervisor and the subordinate. Supervisors view performance reviews as a painful and dreaded task of potentially creating conflict. Subordinates, on the other hand, feel uneasy and uncertain on how the supervisor will rate their performance. This is why performance job reviews fail. It is just too painful for everyone!

A Job Performance Rveiew (JPR) system must be data driven and objective. It also helps if it requires inimal effort for the manager to gather the date and complete the JPR form. Ideally, a supevisor should take less than ten minutes to collect performance data and complete a JPR form. It should be painless.

For the subordinate, the JPR process and rating system must be clearly understood so that they can influence the outcomes. A JPR system must be transparent to the point where the subordinate already knows the general outcome of the JPR

before the scheduled JPR session with their
supervisor.

## Design Considerations

The following factors is best considered in the
development of the JPR system:

- The performance measures for each job
  position supports the department goals.

- Performance data is quick and easy to access.

- Performance standards are clearly defined.

- A manager takes five minutes to gather the
  data and complete a JPR.

- The JPR session is conducted in less than ten
  minutes.

- The JPR ratings is linked to wage adjustments
  or compensation models.

## Rating System

Traditional performance job review review systems
use the academic grading systems of A to F. In
most cases, an A rating means performce meeting
expectation. The academic rating scale will result in
a skewed distribution curve where the average or

mean is positioned on one end of the curve, as shown below.

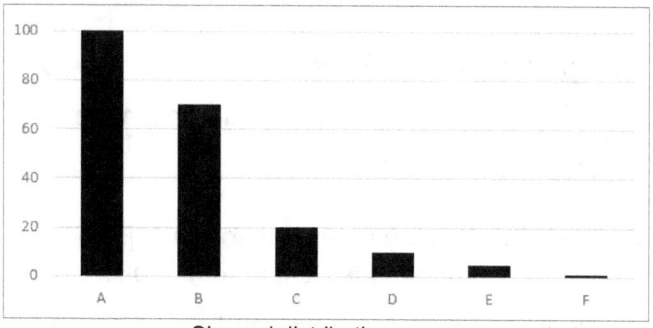
Skewed distribution curve

Unfortunately, the academic rating scale doesn't recognize performance beyond expectation. High performers are lumped together with people performing to standard levels of expectation.

Statistically, human performance follow the normal distribution curve, or bell shape curve, where the majority of the people perform close to the expected performance standard. Occassionally, there will be individuals performing at outstanding levels and others performing below expectations.

The normal distribution curve is a reslistic representation of a fair JPR rating system. Majority of the people perform close to the standard with minimal variations. Only a few individuals are at the high and low ends of the rating scale.

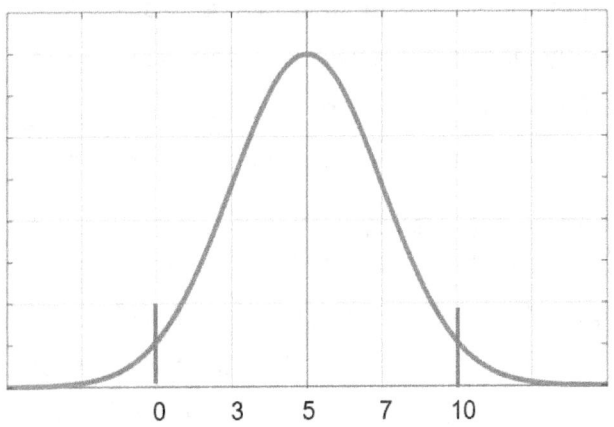

JPR Rating Scale - Normal distribution curve

Using the normal distribution curve rating scale, the rating of 5 means performance meeting expectation. A rating of 1 to 4 is still acceptable, but will require improvement. A rating 6 to 10 indicates performance exceeding expectation.

## JPR Rating Scale – Normal Distribution Curve

**Change Required** (Rating = 0)
The individual fails to deliver the expected performance. Documentation is required to support this rating. The manager increases the JPR frequency, such as monthly or even weekly, to closely mentor the individual to standard performance. Disciplinary action or the the warning process for termination is initiated at this rating.

**Contributing** (Rating = 1 to 4)
The individual performs below the standards of expectation. Documentation is required to support this rating. The supervisor may identify areas for improvement or increase the review frequency to mentor the individual to standard performance.

**Expected** (Rating = 5)
The individual performs to standards or meets expected outcomes. This is the starting point of the rating scale. This is the only rating that does not require any performance documentation.

**Commendable** (Rating = 6 to 9)
The individual consistently performs beyond the standards on a month-to-month basis. Documentation is required to support this rating.

**Exceptional** (Rating = 10)
The individual consistently exceeds the established standards of performance on a year-to-year basis. This is a rare rating to award. Documentation is required to support this rating.

## Components of a Job Performance Review

A JPR document will contain the following:

1.  **List of performance measures**: A list of performance measures, the definition of each performance measure, and sources of data.

2.  **Rating sheet:** A graduated scale of outcomes and the corresponding rating.

3.  **Performance summary**: Rating of each performance item, noting the associated documentation to support the rating above and below the Expected (5) level.

### Performance Measures

Performance measures are not limited to items that directly impact an individual. Total company, department, and team performance need to be considered.

Most performance measures are identified in the team meeting area. You can use team performance measures and account for the individual effort. Here is an example:

*Nonconformances (1) Team*
                *(2) Individual*

Also consider process-compliance and process-improvement items. Supervisors can collect observations and use these as performance data.

# Example Performance Measures

## *Department and Company Performance Measures*

### 1. On-Time Delivery
Definition: Product delivery to customer on or before the due date.

Source of data: Monthly service-level report.

### 2. Productivity
Definition: Total units produced per labor hour.

Source of data: Shop-floor management data.

### 3. Customer Feedback
Definition: Performance feedback from customers.

Source of data: Customer feedback and customer incident reports.

*Individual Performance Measures*
### 4. Internal Defects
Definition: Defects reported by rewind or folder-gluer operations.

Source of data: Scrap form completed by finishing department.

### 5. Productivity
Definition: Total shift good footage produced per labor hour.

Source of data: Shop-floor management data.

### 6. Compliance to Policy and Procedure
Definition: Compliance with corporate and department policies, guidelines, directives, and procedures.

Source of data: Exceptional and substandard performance documented by the supervisor or manager.

## Performance Standards

Standards of performance can be gathered based on historical data or a cascade from the department goal. Make sure the goals are attainable.

## Rating Sheet

A graduated scale of performance outcomes lists the appropriate rating for each item. This will make it easy for the manager to provide an objective and consistent rating. Here is an example:

| Item | Outcome | Rating |
|---|---|---|
| Nonconformance reports (NCRs) | Additional NCRs | −1 for each |
| | 2 NCRs | 5 |
| | 0 NCRs | +1 for every quarter |

# Example JPR Rating Sheet

| | Performance Standards | Value | Rating |
|---|---|---|---|
| 1 | On-time Delivery | 100% | 10 |
| | | 99% | 7 |
| | | 98% | 5 |
| | | 97% | 3 |
| | | 96% | 0 |

| | | | |
|---|---|---|---|
| 2 | Department Productivity | 2200 | 10 |
| | | 1900 | 7 |
| | | 1600 | 5 |
| | | 1500 | 3 |
| | | 1400 | 0 |

| | | | |
|---|---|---|---|
| 3 | Customer Feedback | 0 | 10 |
| | | 5 | 7 |
| | | 10 | 5 |
| | | 15 | 3 |
| | | 20 | 0 |

| | | | |
|---|---|---|---|
| 4 | Internal Defects | 3 Y with 0 | 10 |
| | | 1 Y with 0 | 7 |
| | | 3 | 5 |
| | | 6 | 3 |
| | | 9 | 0 |

| | | | |
|---|---|---|---|
| 5 | Individual Productivity | See Machine Center Standards Sheet | 10 |
| | | | 7 |
| | | | 5 |
| | | | 4 - 3 |
| | | | 0 |

| | | | |
|---|---|---|---|
| 6 | Compliance with Policy & Procedure | ++ | 10 |
| | | + | 7 |
| | | 0 | 5 |
| | | 1 – 2 UO | 4 - 3 |
| | | 3 UO | 0 |

# Example Performance Summary

Name                                        JPR Review
                                              Period _____
_____

| | Rating | Weight | Score | Supporting Data |
|---|---|---|---|---|
| 1. On-time Delivery | | 2 | | |
| 2. Department Productivity | | 2 | | |
| 3. Customer Feedback | | 1 | | |
| 4. Internal Defects | | 1 | | |
| 5. Individual Productivity | | 1 | | |
| 6. Compliance with Policy & Procedure | | 1 | | |
| Sum of Column | | 8 | | |
| Overall JPR Rating | | | | |

Signatures

_____        _____        _____
Employee                   Supervisor              HR Manager

## Completing a JPR Form

Use the rating scale to reference the performance outcome and determine the JPR rating for each item. List supporting documents to justify a rating above or below the Expected (5) level. Write down any additional facts in the Notes section.

Calculate the total JPR rating for the period. Keep in mind that a rating of Expected (5) is a positive rating.

## Review Process

Supervisors should realize that a JPR session is a historical review of performance data. The employee review should be scheduled for no more than ten minutes. Discussion regarding work issues or future job roles should be scheduled separately.

During the performance review, compare performance data with the set goals and objectives. In most cases, items meeting expectation (with a 5 rating) are discussed quickly. Items above and below the Expected (5) level will require a short discussion.

## Linking JPR to Compensation

Translating an individual performance review into a numerical value provides the means for developing a compensation model for wage adjustments or bonuses.

In a wage-adjustment model, an organization develops a percentage distribution, as shown below:

| Rating | Increase |
|---|---|
| 7 and above | 6% |
| 6 | 5% |
| 5 | 4% |
| 4 | 3% |
| 3 and below | 0% |

The distribution scale is applied to current employee wages in determining the total wage adjustments. The calculated total is compared to the budgeted amount, and the scale is adjusted up or down until the budgeted amount is matched.

## Implementation

Implementation of a JPR system requires deliberate planning and execution. The implementation is a learning process for the entire company and requires patience from the supervisor and team members.

The implementation plan requires the supervisor and subordinates to develop the system jointly. This makes the JPR process transparent to the entire company and helps eliminate people's fear of JPRs.

## Example Implementation Timetable

| | |
|---|---|
| Week 1 | Identify job positions |
| Week 2 | Define performance measures |
| Week 3 | Define rating worksheet |
| Week 4 | Develop JPR documents |
| Week 5 | Conduct employee overview |
| Weeks 6–8 | Conduct first trial |
| Week 9 | Review first trial |
| Weeks 9–12 | Conduct second trial |
| Week 13 | Review second trial |
| Weeks 14–17 | Conduct third trial |
| Week 18 | Review third trial |
| Week 19 | Launch JPR systems |

# Bibliography

# Bibliography

Imai, M. Gemba Kaizen: A Common-Sense Approach to a Continuous Improvement Strategy. McGraw-Hill Education. 2012

Japan Management Association and Lu, D. Kanban Just-in Time at Toyota: Management Begins at the Workplace. Productivity Press. 1989

Ohno, T. Toyota Production System: Beyond Large-Scale Production. Productivity Press. 1988.

Shingo S. and Dillon A. A Study of the Toyota Production System: From an Industrial Engineering Viewpoint. Productivity Press. 1989.

Suzaki, K. The New Shop Floor Management: Empowering People for Continuous Improvement. Free Press. 2010.

# Index

# Index

**5**
5S · 55, 56, 57, 64

**A**
Arena of Competition · 71

**B**
Business Process Mapping · 78

**C**
Common Goal · 91
Communication and Support Structure · 43
Compliance · 77, 92, 117, 119, 120
Connector symbol · 86
Contingency · 67, 76
Continuous Improvement · 92
CorPlan · 66
Corporate Planning · 66
corrective action · 3, 7, 28, 30, 39, 43, 45, 49, 79, 96

**D**
Data Integrity · 77
Decision symbol · 85, 89
Diagnostic Measures · 96, 97
Diagnostics measures · 94

**E**
Environmental Analysis · 73

**F**
Fire-Fighting Index · 12
flow control · 58, 59, 60, 61, 102, 103, 104

**H**
Hawthorne Effect · 99

**I**
Input-Process-Output · 91, 92

**J**
JPR · 9, 47, 48, 110, 111, 112, 113, 114, 115, 119, 120, 121, 122, 123

**K**
Kaizen · 99, 100, 101, 102, 103, 104, 106
Kaizen Event · 32
Kaizen Events · 100
Kanban · 58, 59, 60, 61, 62, 63, 102
Key Points · 82, 89, 90

**L**
Lean · i, 65
Line Connector · 83, 85

**M**
Main Steps · 82, 89
Management by Performance Objectives · 45
Management Review · 94, 95

Market Opportunities & Threats · 74
Mission Statement · 69

**O**

Objective · 67, 74, 103
Organization Strengths & Limitations · 71

**P**

PDCA · 6, 49, 50, 51, 52, 53, 99, 103, 105, 106, 107, 108, 109
PDCA Cycle · 49, 50, 52
performance data · 116, 121
performance measures · 91, 111, 115, 116, 123
Performance Metrics · 91, 94, 95, 97, 98
Performance Metrics and Standards · 41
Process capability · 31
Process Compliance · 6, 22, 55, 116
Process Flow · 80, 81, 83, 86
process flow charts · 5, 35, 38
Process Flow Control · 58
Process stability · 24, 25
Process symbol · 84, 85, 86
Process Validation · 15
Program · 67

**Q**

Quality Systems · iii, 94, 96, 98

**R**

Rapid Small

Improvements · 29
Regulatory Affairs · 94, 96, 98
Resource Assessment · 70

**S**

Safety · 89, 94, 96, 98
strategic cascade · 34, 38, 41, 45, 79
strategic plan · 65
Strategic Plan · 65, 66, 67, 74, 76, 77, 94
Strategic Planning · iii, 65, 67, 77
Strategic Rationale · 33
strategic-cascade · 4, 5, 8, 93
Strategy · 65, 67, 75
Suggestions · 92
Support Staff · 103
System · 111
System Thinking · 18

**T**

Terminator · 83
Think small · 30
Total Quality Management · 65
Toyota Production System · 2, 5, 34, 55
Training Method · 90

**U**

Undesired Processes · 88

**V**

visual controls · 45, 64

**W**

Work Instructions · 80
Workflow Schematic · 14